AF (adverb)

Definition: Intensely, extremely, or to the max. It's like the exclamation point of slang.
Usage: Used to exaggerate how much you feel or relate to something.

Example:
"That new Marvel movie was boring AF. I fell asleep halfway through."
Tip: Replace "very" in any sentence with "AF" and suddenly you're cooler. But remember, overusing it is cringe AF.

And I Oop (phrase)

Definition: A playful expression of shock, surprise, or realization. Think of it as the verbal equivalent of a double take.
Usage: Ideal for reacting to awkward moments or when someone accidentally spills the tea.

Examples:
"She said what about her ex? And I oop!"
Accidentally drops your iced coffee "And I oop..."

Fun Fact: *This phrase went viral thanks to drag queen Jasmine Masters, proving that one can become iconic by simply reacting to life.*

Aesthetic (noun)

Definition: A vibe, style, or carefully curated look. It's not just fashion—it's a lifestyle.
Usage: Use to compliment someone's ability to look effortlessly cool or to describe your Instagram theme.

Examples:
"Her whole cottagecore aesthetic makes me want to buy a farm."
"I'm going for a Y2K aesthetic with my outfit today. Thoughts?"

Tip: Pair this with subgenres like "dark academia" or "e-girl" to sound extra refined. Bonus points if you say it with a slightly pretentious tone.

Attacc (verb)

Definition: A meme-inspired way to say "attack," often in a funny or exaggerated context.
Usage: Perfect for describing any over-the-top or cartoonish act of aggression.

Examples:

"My dog saw the delivery guy and immediately went to attacc."

"Someone called me basic, so I had to verbally attacc."

Fun Fact: Often paired with "he protec" in memes because balance is important—even in internet humor.

Alive, but barely (phrase)

Definition: A dramatic way of saying you're exhausted, overwhelmed, or just done with life, but still somehow functioning.

Usage: Often used in response to questions like "How are you?" when you're not fine.

Examples:

"Finals week? I'm alive, but barely."

"After leg day at the gym, I'm alive, but barely."

Pro Tip: Bonus effect if you say it with a slight groan for maximum pity points.

Adulting (noun/verb)

Definition: The act of doing boring, grown-up tasks like paying bills, grocery shopping, or scheduling a dentist appointment.

Usage: When you're proud of yourself for doing something responsible, but also sad about it.

Examples:
"I remembered to do laundry this week. Adulting level: expert."
"Ugh, I hate adulting. Why do we have to pay rent every month?"
Fun Fact: Millennials started this term, but Gen Z kept it alive because adulting still sucks.

B

Bet (interjection)
Definition: An enthusiastic agreement or confirmation. Think of it as "okay," but with extra energy and confidence.
Usage: Perfect for accepting plans, challenges, or agreements with a little flair.

Examples:
"You down for a Taco Bell run at midnight?"
"Bet."
"I can totally beat you in Mario Kart."
"Bet, let's go!"
Synonyms: "Deal," "sure thing."

Origin: Popularized by Atlanta rap culture and made universal by TikTok.

Bussin' (adjective)

Definition: Delicious, amazing, or top-tier, often referring to food but can also describe anything impressive.
Usage: Throw it out when something tastes so good, it feels illegal.

Examples:
"This mac and cheese is bussin' bussin'. Did you make it from scratch?"
"That new boba spot? Bussin', no cap."
Related Phrase: "Leaving no crumbs"—when someone's performance or cooking is flawless.

Bread (noun)

Definition: Money, wealth, or anything that makes your wallet happier.
Usage: For anyone grinding, hustling, or making moves to get paid.

Examples:
"I gotta secure that bread so I can buy concert tickets."

"Quit your job? How are you gonna get your bread now?"
Bonus Category – Usage Expansion:
Break Bread (phrase): To share money or resources generously.
Example: "She's always willing to break bread with her friends."

Big Yikes (noun)

Definition: A supersized reaction to cringe-worthy, awkward, or disastrous situations. Like "yikes," but with a little more spice.
Usage: When something is so embarrassing it makes you want to run away for the person involved.

Examples:
"He proposed at a baseball game, and she said no. Big yikes."
"You wore Crocs to prom? Big yikes."
Category – Opposite Term:
Small Yikes (phrase): Reserved for mildly awkward situations.
Example: "Forgot to mute yourself on Zoom? Small yikes."

Bougie (adjective)

Definition: Acting fancy, pretentious, or high-class, often in an ironic way.
Usage: Can be used positively or negatively, depending on context.

Examples:
"She refuses to drink coffee unless it's oat milk lattes. So bougie."
"We're eating steak tonight. Look at us being all bougie!"
Origins: Derived from "bourgeoisie," but now it just means you're trying too hard to be fancy.

Bye Felicia (phrase)

Definition: A dismissive way of saying goodbye to someone who's irrelevant, annoying, or unnecessary in the moment.
Usage: The perfect phrase for when you're done with someone or something.

Examples:
"You're really arguing over pineapple on pizza? Bye Felicia."
"They tried to cancel boba on Twitter. Bye Felicia."
Pop Culture Note: Originated from the 1995 movie Friday, but it's now part of the Gen Z clapback arsenal.

C

Cap/No Cap (noun/phrase)

Definition:Cap: A lie, exaggeration, or falsehood.
No Cap: Complete honesty, the truth, or facts only.
Usage: To call someone out for lying or confirm you're telling the truth.

Examples:
"You said you can bench 300 pounds? That's cap."
"This new game is the best thing ever, no cap."
Tip: Add "fr" (short for "for real") after "no cap" for maximum emphasis.
Example: "No cap, this pizza is bussin', fr."

Caught in 4K (phrase)

Definition: Exposed or caught red-handed, with undeniable evidence (usually video or screenshots).
Usage: Ideal for dragging someone who's been less than sneaky.

Examples:
"He said he was at home, but we caught him in 4K on Snapchat at the party."

"Don't delete your comment, we've got the receipts—you're caught in 4K."
Fun Fact: Inspired by the clarity of 4K resolution, because if you're going to be caught, might as well be in HD.

CEO of [something] (noun)

Definition: Someone who's the best at or embodies something (often sarcastic).
Usage: Crown someone with this unofficial title for excelling (or failing) at a specific trait.

Examples:
"She's the CEO of being late to everything."
"Wow, you're the CEO of making awkward jokes at family dinners."
Fun Fact: This started as a Twitter meme where people self-declared their expertise in the most random things.

Chill (adjective/verb)

Definition:
Adjective: Relaxed, easygoing, or unproblematic.
Verb: To hang out, relax, or vibe with no agenda.
Usage: Often used to describe people, activities, or the general mood.

Examples:

"She's super chill—she never gets mad about anything."

"We're just chilling at my place tonight, nothing big."

Tip: If someone says "be chill," it's code for "don't make this weird."

Cringe (adjective/noun)

Definition: Something painfully awkward, embarrassing, or try-hard. It's the ultimate label of disapproval.

Usage: Used to roast bad behavior, awkward moments, or outdated trends.

Examples:

"Did he just dab unironically? Cringe."

"Posting your breakup on Instagram? That's peak cringe."

Fun Fact: Gen Z uses "cringe" to describe anything that disrupts their constant pursuit of effortless coolness.

Clown (noun/verb)

Definition: A person who embarrasses themselves or gets played, often by ignoring obvious red flags.

Usage: Perfect for self-roasting or calling someone out.

Examples:

"I thought he liked me, but he ghosted me. Guess I'm the clown."

"You went back to your ex again? Clown behavior."

Category – Emoji Connection:

The emoji is shorthand for calling someone a clown.

Example: "Me thinking I'd save money this month ."

D

Dank (adjective)

Definition: Extremely cool, edgy, or high-quality, often used to describe memes, jokes, or internet content.

Usage: Use it to compliment something so absurdly funny it feels illegal.

Examples:

"That cat meme you sent? So dank, I had to show everyone."

"He told a joke so dank I nearly fell off my chair."

Category – Origins: Borrowed from stoner slang, where "dank" originally referred to high-quality marijuana, but now it's a badge of honor for top-tier memes.

Dead (adjective)

Definition: A state of being metaphorically deceased due to something being hilariously funny or absurd.
Usage: For situations when "LOL" just doesn't cut it.

Examples:
"She walked into the wrong Zoom meeting and presented to the wrong class. I'm dead."
"That TikTok about pets narrating their lives? Dead."
Fun Fact: Black Twitter popularized this term, proving that laughter is the best way to describe your demise.

Drip (noun)

Definition: Stylish clothing or accessories that exude confidence and swag.
Usage: The go-to word for complimenting someone's outfit when "cool" feels too basic.

Examples:
"Those sneakers? Straight drip."
"Look at her walking into the room with that designer bag. Drip everywhere!"
Tip: Saying "dripping harder than a leaky faucet" will get you bonus style points—or eye-rolls.

Dragged (verb)

Definition: Publicly roasted, criticized, or humiliated—often in a savage but funny way.
Usage: Happens when someone's bad opinion or poor behavior is torn apart online.

Examples:
"She tried to gatekeep iced coffee and got dragged on Twitter."
"That actor's bad apology video? He's getting dragged in the comments."
Category – Emoji Usage: The 🔥 (fire) emoji often accompanies "dragged" because a good roast should burn.

Doomscrolling (verb)

Definition: The act of endlessly scrolling through bad news or depressing content online, even though it's terrible for your mental health.
Usage: Perfect for late-night social media binges that leave you spiraling.

Examples:
"I spent three hours doomscrolling about climate change last night. Send snacks and therapy."
"You're still reading tweets about the breakup drama? Stop doomscrolling."

Tip: Gen Z knows doomscrolling is bad but does it anyway. Self-awareness doesn't always help.

DIY'd the Heck Out of It (phrase)

Definition: To make or do something yourself in an overly elaborate or creative way, often as a solution to a problem.
Usage: For any moment of excessive craftiness or ingenuity.

Examples:
"She DIY'd the heck out of her prom dress with glue and sequins."
"Ran out of coffee filters, so I used a paper towel. DIY'd the heck out of my morning."
Category – Relatable Humor: Gen Z loves a good DIY because it's both resourceful and chaotic.

E

E-boy/E-girl (noun)

Definition: A highly curated online persona with a blend of emo, alternative, and trendy vibes.
Usage: Use when someone looks like they live for TikTok fame and eyeliner wings.

Examples:

"That guy with the chain necklaces and painted nails? Definitely an E-boy."

"She's got green hair and a thrifted sweater—total E-girl vibes."

Tip: Bonus points if they're dramatically lip-syncing sad songs into their phones.

Extra (adjective)

Definition: Over-the-top, dramatic, or putting in more effort than necessary.

Usage: Call someone "extra" when they go all out, whether it's warranted or not.

Examples:

"He made a playlist and themed decorations for a casual hangout. So extra."

"Her outfit today? Five-inch heels at the farmer's market? Extra."

Fun Fact: Being extra is sometimes an insult, but let's be real—extra people are the life of the party.

Explaining the Joke (phrase)

Definition: The act of killing humor by over-explaining why something is funny.
Usage: Happens when someone doesn't get a meme and ruins it for everyone.

Examples:
"Wait, so the dog's wearing a hat because... Ugh, never mind, you're explaining the joke."
"Stop explaining that meme. It was funny until you talked."
Category – Don't Be That Person: If someone says, "I guess you had to be there," they've already lost.

Eat (or Eating) (verb)

Definition: To excel or perform exceptionally, often with flair. It's all about serving confidence and results.
Usage: For moments when someone dominates the stage, the runway, or even a dinner plate.

Examples:
"She's eating this choreography—look at her go!"
"That speech? He ate and left no crumbs."
Category – Culinary Metaphor: Gen Z makes success sound delicious. Who doesn't want to leave no crumbs?

Energizer Bunny Moment (phrase)

Definition: A burst of endless energy, often surprising and out of nowhere.
Usage: Use when someone keeps going when everyone else is ready to crash.

Examples:
"He studied for 10 hours straight. Total Energizer Bunny moment."
"We're all tired, but she's still dancing. Energizer Bunny mode activated."
Tip: Add a sarcastic tone if the energy is too much.

F

Finsta (noun)

Definition: A "fake Instagram" account used to post chaotic, unfiltered, or deeply personal content, usually for a small circle of close friends.
Usage: The place where you can be your most unhinged self, away from prying eyes.

Examples:
"My finsta is full of bad selfies and late-night rants. No one but my besties is allowed."
"I posted a crying video on my finsta. It's been that kind of week."

Fun Fact: Your finsta is where you go to be real, while your main Insta is for flexing and curated content.

Flex (verb/noun)

Definition:
(verb) To show off or brag about something.
(noun) The thing being shown off, whether it's deserved or not.
Usage: Often used sarcastically for minor achievements.

Examples:
"He's flexing his new AirPods like we haven't all seen them before."
"Getting eight hours of sleep is a flex these days."
Category – Reverse Flex: Self-deprecating flexing is a Gen Z specialty.
Example: "I did the dishes today. Huge flex, I know."

FYP (noun)

Definition: The "For You Page" on TikTok, a personalized feed where the algorithm delivers videos tailored to your every interest.
Usage: Refers not only to TikTok's main feature but also to the magic of its hyper-targeted content.

Examples:

"My FYP knows me better than I know myself."

"How did a cooking video land on my FYP? I can't even make toast."

Tip: Don't fight the algorithm. If your FYP is all cat videos and existential memes, lean in—it knows what you need.

Fire (adjective)

Definition: Amazing, impressive, or exceptionally good. The highest praise for music, fashion, or basically anything.

Usage: A versatile compliment for things that slap.

Examples:

"This playlist is fire. Who made it?"

"Your jacket is so fire, I might steal it."

Fun Fact: Gen Z loves heat-based slang—fire is cool, but mid is lukewarm.

Flop (noun/verb)

Definition:

(noun) Something that fails spectacularly.

(verb) To fail or not live up to expectations.

Usage: Whether it's a movie, a trend, or someone's bad attempt at flirting, flop covers it all.

Examples:
"That celebrity tried to make NFTs happen, but it was a total flop."
"I studied for hours, but I still flopped on that test."
Category – Opposite Term:
Serve: When someone exceeds expectations.
Example: "Her speech? Not a flop—it was a serve."

Facts (interjection)

Definition: A way to agree with or validate a statement. Short for "That's a fact."
Usage: Use it when someone says something so true it doesn't even need discussion.

Examples:
"Pizza rolls are the superior snack. Facts."
"That show really fell off after season two. Facts."
Tip: Adding "big" before "facts" increases your conviction.
Example: "Pineapple on pizza? Big facts."

G

Glow Up (noun/verb)

Definition: A dramatic transformation for the better, whether it's physical, emotional, or personal. Think of it as an evolution from awkward to thriving.
Usage: Use it to describe someone who's living their best life post-puberty, breakup, or bad haircut.

Examples:
"She had such a glow up after high school—who is this supermodel?"
"I've been working out and eating clean for my glow up arc."
Fun Fact: Glow-ups are often paired with throwback photos for maximum "look how far I've come" energy.

Goated (adjective)

Definition: The greatest of all time (G.O.A.T.). A term of the highest praise, reserved for legends, icons, and peak excellence.
Usage: Use it to crown anything from people to food to memes.

Examples:
"Beyoncé? Goated."
"This ramen place? Goated on the sticks."

Tip: Adding "on the sticks" is TikTok slang for something dominating in its field. It originated in gaming but works for anything.

Gaslighting (verb)

Definition: Manipulating someone into doubting their reality or perceptions. Often used to describe toxic behavior, but also jokingly in minor disagreements. Usage: For calling out someone's sneaky attempts to rewrite history.

Examples:
"She said she never borrowed my hoodie? Stop gaslighting me—it's right there!"
"You told me we were meeting at 6 PM, don't try to gaslight me now."
Fun Fact: The term comes from the 1944 film Gaslight, where a husband manipulates his wife by dimming the lights and denying it. Creepy, right?

Gucci (adjective)

Definition: A synonym for "cool," "fine," or "all good." It's basically the chill cousin of "fire."
Usage: Use it to describe a situation, mood, or vibe that's smooth and unproblematic.

Examples:

"How's the group project going?"

"It's Gucci—everyone's doing their part."

"You're good with the plan?"

"Gucci."

Tip: Don't overuse it unless you're prepared to sound like a wannabe hypebeast.

Ghosting (verb)

Definition: The act of cutting off communication with someone without warning or explanation. Usually occurs in dating but applies to friendships, too.

Usage: Perfect for when someone disappears mid-conversation or after a few dates.

Examples:

"We were texting every day, and then he just ghosted me."

"I thought we were cool, but she ghosted me after the group project ended."

Category – Opposite Term:

Haunting (verb): When someone you ghosted starts liking your old posts or sliding back into your DMs.

Example: "He ghosted me last year, but now he's haunting my Instagram."

Gassing Someone Up (verb)

Definition: Hyping someone up, boosting their confidence, or showering them with compliments.
Usage: Use it when you're being the ultimate cheerleader for your friends.

Examples:
"She was nervous about her speech, so we gassed her up beforehand."
"You're killing it in that outfit. Let me gas you up real quick!"
Tip: Gassing someone up is all about good vibes. Overdo it, though, and they might think you're sarcastic.

H

Hits Different (phrase)

Definition: Describes something that feels uniquely impactful or emotional in a specific context.
Usage: Often paired with music, nostalgic moments, or random experiences that strike a chord.

Examples:

"This song hits different when you're walking alone at night."

"Drinking hot chocolate on a snowy day? It just hits different."

Tip: Say it dramatically for maximum main character vibes.

Highkey/Lowkey (adverbs)

Definition:

Highkey: Openly or obviously; with full enthusiasm.

Lowkey: Subtly or secretly; with understated energy.

Usage: Perfect for expressing the full spectrum of excitement.

Examples:

"I highkey need a vacation right now."

"I lowkey think pineapple on pizza is amazing."

Fun Fact: Combining both in one sentence is peak Gen Z chaos.

Example: "I lowkey hate her but highkey want to borrow her jacket."

Hard Launch (noun)

Definition: The bold, unmistakable act of publicly announcing a relationship, usually with a couple's photo or post on social media.
Usage: It's the digital equivalent of shouting "We're official!" from the rooftops.

Examples:
"Posted a pic with bae holding hands—hard launch achieved."
"I skipped the soft launch and went straight to a hard launch with that selfie."
Category – Opposite Term:
Soft Launch (noun): Subtle hints about a relationship without revealing too much.
Example: "She soft launched her new boyfriend with a picture of their shoes."

Hella (adjective/adverb)

Definition: Extremely, very, or a lot of something. The West Coast's gift to the English language.
Usage: Use it to emphasize just how much you're feeling or experiencing something.

Examples:
"That party last night was hella fun."
"I'm hella tired, but let's do this."

Fun Fact: Hella originated in Northern California slang and somehow conquered the world—or at least TikTok.

Haunted (adjective)

Definition: When a past experience, memory, or mistake lingers in your mind, usually to torment you.
Usage: For those cringe-worthy moments you can't stop replaying in your head.

Examples:
"I'm haunted by the time I accidentally called my teacher 'mom.'"
"Her old tweets are haunting her during job interviews."
Tip: It's less about ghosts and more about emotional baggage.

Hater Energy (phrase)

Definition: A vibe of negativity, jealousy, or unnecessary criticism. Often used to call out someone trying to dim your shine.
Usage: Perfect for shutting down trolls, critics, or anyone raining on your parade.

Examples:

"She said my outfit was 'too much.' That's some hater energy."

"Don't bring hater energy into this group chat."

Pro Tip: Combat hater energy with relentless self–confidence—or memes.

I

IYKYK (phrase)

Definition: "If You Know, You Know." Refers to an inside joke, shared experience, or niche reference that only a select few will understand.

Usage: Ideal for flexing your membership in an exclusive club of knowledge.

Examples:

"The way we left that party early... IYKYK."

"That joke about the vending machine? IYKYK."

Fun Fact: This phrase is essentially the secret handshake of the internet.

It's Giving [something] (phrase)

Definition: Used to describe the vibe or energy something or someone embodies. Can be sincere, sarcastic, or over-the-top dramatic.

Usage: Often followed by hyper-specific descriptions.

Examples:
"That blazer? It's giving CEO energy."
"This weather? It's giving 'sad main character in a romantic movie.'"
Tip: Use for maximum impact when combined with outlandish comparisons.
Example: "Her outfit is giving 'alien queen meets 2005 prom.'"

I'm Dead (phrase)

Definition: A dramatic response to something hilariously funny or absurd. It's the verbal equivalent of rolling on the floor laughing.
Usage: Replace "LOL" with this for moments that leave you metaphorically deceased.

Examples:
"He slipped on a banana peel in front of everyone. I'm dead."
"That meme of cats with wigs? Dead."
Category – Related Terms:
Deceased: An elevated version of "dead."
Example: "That comeback? I'm deceased."

In My Feels (phrase)

Definition: A state of being deeply emotional, nostalgic, or reflective. Usually hits late at night or when listening to sad music.
Usage: For moments when you're overwhelmed by your emotions, whether they're happy, sad, or bittersweet.

Examples:
"I was looking at old photos last night, and I was in my feels."
"This song put me in my feels. Why does Adele do this to me?"
Tip: Play some Lana Del Rey or Frank Ocean for maximum feels.

It's the [something] for Me (phrase)

Definition: A way to highlight the standout feature of a situation, person, or thing. Can be used positively or negatively.
Usage: Use this phrase to roast, compliment, or just state what caught your attention.

Examples:

"It's the confidence for me. She just walked into the room like she owned it."

"It's the spelling errors for me. Proofread your texts!"

Fun Fact: This phrase became a viral roast format on TikTok, evolving into an all-purpose observation tool.

Iconic (adjective)

Definition: Something so remarkable, unique, or unforgettable that it deserves a place in the pop culture hall of fame.

Usage: A high compliment for standout people, moments, or even memes.

Examples:

"That outfit? Iconic."

"His performance was iconic—everyone's talking about it."

Tip: Use sparingly; not everything is truly iconic. Save it for the Beyoncé-level moments.

J

JOMO (noun)

Definition: The "Joy of Missing Out," where you genuinely enjoy skipping social events and opting for peace, comfort, or me-time instead.

Usage: Perfect for introverts, or anyone too tired to fake small talk.

Examples:
"I stayed in with my blanket and snacks instead of going to that party. JOMO vibes."
"Everyone's posting about Coachella, but I've got JOMO. No crowds, no stress."
Tip: JOMO is the antidote to FOMO. Embrace it unapologetically.

Just Vibes (phrase)

Definition: Living in the moment, embracing chill energy, and not stressing about anything serious.
Usage: Often used when hanging out with no plans, or when life is simply about enjoying the atmosphere.

Examples:
"We're just sitting by the beach with snacks. No drama, just vibes."
"The road trip playlist is fire—this whole day is just vibes."
Fun Fact: "Just vibes" is basically the philosophy of Gen Z in three words.

Juicy (adjective)

Definition: Describes something exciting, dramatic, or full of intrigue—especially gossip or rumors.
Usage: Use it to hype up the tea before spilling it.

Examples:
"You won't believe what happened at the party. It's so juicy."
"I heard some juicy details about her new boyfriend."
Category – Gossip Tier Levels:
Juicy > Scandalous > Spicy
Example: "Juicy is the gateway; scandalous is the full drama show."

Janky (adjective)

Definition: Low-quality, broken, or just plain sketchy. Can describe everything from faulty gadgets to shady plans.
Usage: When something's functionality (or vibe) feels off.

Examples:
"This old laptop is so janky it shuts down randomly."
"He's driving us in a car with no brakes? That's janky as hell."
Tip: Bonus points if you use "janky" to roast something that's trying way too hard to seem legit.

Juiced (adjective)

Definition: Excited, hyped, or full of energy for something. The verbal version of fist-pumping.
Usage: Perfect for pre-event enthusiasm or celebrating wins.

Examples:
"I'm so juiced for this concert tonight. It's gonna be epic."
"Our team won the game, and everyone's juiced!"
Fun Fact: Though it can sound like a sports term, it's become universal for any moment of pure adrenaline.

Jokes on You (phrase)

Definition: A playful or sarcastic comeback to point out irony, usually when someone's attempt to tease backfires.
Usage: Throw it out when you've got the upper hand.

Examples:
"You thought I was embarrassed? Jokes on you, I own this chaos."
"He said I couldn't dance, but jokes on you—I wasn't trying to!"
Category – Add-On:

Pair it with for extra roasting power.
Example: "Jokes on you , I am the clown."

K

Karen (noun)

Definition: A term used to describe someone (usually middle-aged) who is entitled, demanding, or prone to unnecessary drama, especially in public or customer service settings.
Usage: The ultimate insult for anyone who says, "I'd like to speak to the manager."

Examples:
"She called the cops on kids selling lemonade? Total Karen move."
"He's arguing with the waiter about soup temperature? Karen energy."
Category – Related Terms:
Kevin: The male equivalent of a Karen.
Example: "He's being such a Kevin about the Wi-Fi not working."

Kicking It (verb)

Definition: Relaxing, hanging out, or spending time casually. No pressure, no plans, just vibes.
Usage: Use when describing any chill gathering or activity.

Examples:
"We're just kicking it at my place tonight. Come over."
"We kicked it by the pool all afternoon, doing absolutely nothing."
Tip: Saying "kicking it old school" adds a retro twist for reminiscing about simpler times.

Killed It (phrase)

Definition: To perform exceptionally well or succeed beyond expectations.
Usage: Can apply to anything from nailing a presentation to dominating karaoke night.

Examples:
"She absolutely killed it on stage tonight. Standing ovation!"
"That homemade lasagna? You killed it, chef."
Fun Fact: The phrase is versatile—just make sure to clarify context so no one thinks you're confessing to a crime.

Keeping It 100 (phrase)

Definition: Staying honest, real, or authentic—no sugarcoating, no filters.
Usage: For moments when you're telling it like it is, whether people want to hear it or not.

Examples:
"I'm keeping it 100—your haircut isn't as cool as you think it is."
"She always keeps it 100, even when the truth hurts."
Pro Tip: Pair it with the 💯 emoji for full Gen Z approval.
Example: "That movie was mid, 💯."

Krusty (adjective)

Definition: Gross, tired-looking, or unkempt. A playful way of saying someone (or something) is a bit of a mess.
Usage: Often self-deprecating or used to describe mornings after an all-nighter.

Examples:
"I've been running on three hours of sleep, so I'm feeling krusty today."
"His shoes are so krusty they look older than me."
Fun Fact: "Krusty" can also describe bad vibes or a negative attitude.

Example: "Don't be krusty—just let people enjoy things."

Knocked It Out of the Park (phrase)

Definition: Another way of saying someone excelled or surpassed expectations. Derived from baseball but used universally.
Usage: A classic way to hype up someone's success.

Examples:
"Your pitch at work? You knocked it out of the park. Promotion incoming."
"She knocked it out of the park with her outfit. Literal fashion goals."
Tip: Pair this phrase with a fist bump for extra dad-joke energy.

L

Lewk (noun)

Definition: A carefully curated and fashionable appearance, often bold or statement-making.
Usage: When someone's outfit or vibe is serving energy, not just clothing.

Examples:

"That jacket with those boots? A whole lewk."
"Her festival outfit is giving alien princess. What a lewk!"
Tip: Pronounce it with extra emphasis on the "ew" for maximum effect: "LEWWK."

Living Rent-Free (phrase)

Definition: When something occupies your thoughts constantly, usually without your consent.
Usage: Refers to memes, songs, or even embarrassing moments that won't leave your head.

Examples:
"That TikTok audio lives rent-free in my head."
"Her comeback during the argument? Rent-free in my brain since Tuesday."
Fun Fact: It's the ultimate metaphor for Gen Z's relationship with overthinking.

L (noun)

Definition: Short for "loss," it's used to describe a failure, defeat, or setback. The opposite of a "W" (win).
Usage: Call it an "L" when things don't go your way—or to roast someone else's misfortune.

Examples:

"I forgot my charger and now my phone's dead. Big L."
"He got rejected in front of everyone. That's an L if I've ever seen one."
Tip: Add "huge" or "massive" for emphasis.
Example: "She tripped while holding her coffee. Huge L."

Let's Go (phrase)

Definition: A hype phrase expressing excitement, motivation, or readiness for action.
Usage: Use it for anything from winning a game to starting a road trip.

Examples:
"We just scored front-row tickets to the concert. Let's go!"
"Final exam is over. Let's go!"
Category – Emoji Pairing: Add 🔥 or 🚀 for maximum energy.
Example: "Got the last donut at work. Let's go 🔥!"

Lowkey (adverb)

Definition: Subtly, secretly, or without making a big deal out of it. The opposite of "highkey."
Usage: Use it to downplay your feelings, opinions, or actions.

Examples:

"I lowkey love pineapple on pizza, but I'll never admit it in public."

"She's lowkey the funniest person in our group."

Fun Fact: Saying "lowkey" before a confession softens the blow—or makes it sound sneakier.

Lit (adjective)

Definition: Amazing, exciting, or on fire (figuratively). Used to describe anything fun or hype-worthy.

Usage: Although slightly outdated, still relevant for parties, events, or moments of triumph.

Examples:

"That party last night? So lit."

"Her new song is lit—I've had it on repeat all day."

Tip: Don't mix "lit" with overly formal situations.

Example: "This wedding toast is lit" might not land with Grandma.

M

Main Character Energy (noun)

Definition: Acting as if the world revolves around you in a cinematic way. Often paired with dramatic confidence or over-the-top vibes.
Usage: For those moments when you feel like life is your movie, and everyone else is just an extra.

Examples:
"I walked into that coffee shop like it was a rom-com. Main character energy."
"She gave a whole speech about her breakup in class. Big main character energy."
Tip: Bonus points if you add slow-motion effects in your head.

Mid (adjective)

Definition: Mediocre, average, or not living up to the hype. The ultimate dismissal of anything that doesn't impress.
Usage: Use it to roast overrated trends or express your lack of enthusiasm.

Examples:
"That new superhero movie? Kinda mid, not gonna lie."
"I tried their iced coffee, and it was so mid I didn't even finish it."

Fun Fact: The word's simplicity makes it the ultimate insult—it's not bad enough to hate, just not good enough to care.

Mood (noun)

Definition: A phrase used to describe something deeply relatable or that matches your current energy.
Usage: The perfect way to validate any emotion or vibe, from laziness to chaos.

Examples:
"Eating cereal for dinner? Mood."
"That dog lounging in the sun? Absolute mood."
Category – Amplification: Add "big" or "ultimate" for stronger vibes.
Example: "Falling asleep during a Zoom meeting? Big mood."

Moment (noun)

Definition: A fleeting period of greatness, often used to highlight when someone or something is thriving.
Usage: For calling out anything that's having its time to shine.

Examples:

"That outfit is a total moment. You look amazing."
"Pumpkin spice season? It's having its moment right now."
Fun Fact: Everything can be a "moment," from a trend to a random Tuesday.

Manifesting (verb)

Definition: The act of willing something into existence by thinking or speaking it into reality.
Usage: Often paired with hopes, dreams, or unrealistic crushes.

Examples:
"I'm manifesting good vibes for my job interview tomorrow."
"Let's manifest free tickets to the concert. Positive energy only!"
Category – Accessory Phrase: Pair with ✦ for extra magic.
Example: "Manifesting that my crush notices me ✦."

Messy (adjective)

Definition: Describes chaotic, dramatic, or over-the-top behavior, especially in social situations.
Usage: Can be used as an insult or compliment, depending on the context.

Examples:

"He started flirting with his ex's best friend? So messy."

"You accidentally sent that text to the group chat? Messy, but iconic."

Tip: "Messy" people make life entertaining; embrace the chaos.

N

No Cap (phrase)

Definition: A way to emphasize truth or honesty. The opposite of "cap" (a lie).

Usage: Use it to back up your claims or call out facts.

Examples:

"This pizza is the best I've ever had, no cap."

"He said he could bench 400 pounds? That's definitely cap."

Tip: Add "fr" (for real) for extra truth-telling power.

Example: "No cap, this playlist is fire, fr."

NPC (noun)

Definition: Non-Playable Character; refers to someone who seems generic, robotic, or out of touch—like a background character in a video game.
Usage: For roasting someone who gives off no personality or seems out of sync with the group.

Examples:
"That guy has said the same thing three times today. Total NPC vibes."
"She was just standing at the party staring at the wall. Is she an NPC?"
Fun Fact: First popularized in gaming, but TikTok turned it into the ultimate social critique.

Normalize (verb)

Definition: A call to make something more acceptable or mainstream. Often used ironically to point out things that shouldn't need normalization.
Usage: Perfect for expressing what society needs to chill about.

Examples:
"Normalize saying 'I don't know' instead of pretending to have all the answers."
"Can we normalize showing up to events without a gift? I'm broke."

Category – Sarcasm: Use ironically to point out absurd suggestions.
Example: "Normalize eating dessert for every meal."

Not Me [doing something] (phrase)

Definition: A way to confess or call yourself out on doing something embarrassing, funny, or relatable.
Usage: Used for self-deprecating humor or to acknowledge awkward moments.

Examples:
"Not me accidentally liking his 2015 selfie."
"Not me crying over a commercial about dogs."
Tip: Pair with a 🐻 emoji for maximum self-roast energy.

Next Level (adjective)

Definition: Describes something that's exceptional, innovative, or on a higher plane of existence.
Usage: For hyping up something or someone who's outdone themselves.

Examples:
"This dessert is next level. Is that edible glitter?"
"She came to the party in a dress made of LED lights. Next level."

Fun Fact: Borrowed from gaming, where advancing levels = total domination.

Netflix and Cry (phrase)

Definition: A playful twist on "Netflix and chill," referring to watching emotional movies or shows that leave you sobbing.
Usage: For those nights when you just need a good cry in front of the screen.

Examples:
"I spent last night watching The Notebook. Total Netflix and cry vibes."
"She's binging This Is Us. It's all Netflix and cry over there."
Tip: Stock up on tissues and ice cream beforehand for the full experience.

O

On God (phrase)

Definition: Used to swear sincerity or truth, similar to "I swear" or "for real."
Usage: For doubling down on your statement, especially when no one believes you.

Examples:

"I didn't touch your fries, on God."

"This new game is amazing, on God. You've got to try it."

Tip: Use sparingly to avoid sounding overly defensive—or like you're lying.

Oof (interjection)

Definition: A sound of sympathy, awkwardness, or discomfort. Think of it as a verbal wince.

Usage: Perfect for situations when words fail to express how bad something is.

Examples:

"You got locked out of your apartment? Oof."

"He got roasted by the entire group chat? Big oof."

Fun Fact: "Oof" gained viral popularity from the Roblox death sound, because even video games know the feeling.

Out of Pocket (adjective)

Definition: Acting wild, inappropriate, or completely off the rails.

Usage: Use it to describe behavior that's unexpected or over-the-top.

Examples:

"He showed up to the meeting in pajamas. That's out of pocket."

"She made a joke about my ex? Out of pocket, but I'm laughing."

Category – Levels of Chaos:

Mildly out of pocket: A little bold but forgivable.

Fully out of pocket: Total mayhem.

Obsessed (adjective)

Definition: An exaggerated way of saying you love something, often used for people, outfits, or food.
Usage: For moments when regular enthusiasm won't cut it.

Examples:

"Her new hair color? Obsessed."

"I'm obsessed with this new boba flavor—it's everything."

Tip: Add "literally" before "obsessed" for peak Gen Z emphasis.

Example: "I'm literally obsessed with this song. I've played it 20 times today."

Ok Boomer (phrase)

Definition: A sarcastic clapback used to dismiss outdated opinions, usually from older generations. Usage: Best deployed when someone is being condescending or out of touch.

Examples:
"You don't need another tattoo."
"Ok Boomer."
"Why do you always take pictures of your food?"
"Ok Boomer, chill."
Fun Fact: This phrase became a viral sensation as a response to generational arguments but is now used playfully even between peers.

Own It (phrase)

Definition: To confidently embrace or take responsibility for something, whether it's good or bad. Usage: For moments when someone should lean into their actions or personality.

Examples:
"You made that mistake, so own it and move on."
"She wore Crocs to prom and totally owned it. Iconic."
Tip: Confidence is key. Owning it makes even bad choices seem intentional.

P

Pushin' P (phrase)

Definition: Staying real, keeping things positive, or acting with integrity. Originates from Gunna's song "Pushin' P."
Usage: Use it to praise someone's actions or to describe living your best, most authentic life.

Examples:
"He helped me move on his day off. That's pushin' P."
"We're all about keeping it real and pushin' P around here."
Fun Fact: The "P" is intentionally vague, making it endlessly adaptable—just make sure you're using it in a positive way.

Periodt (interjection)

Definition: A sassy way to emphasize the end of a discussion or to punctuate a statement. Often used to signify that no further argument is needed.
Usage: Works best when delivered with dramatic flair.

Examples:
"She's the best singer in this school, periodt."

"If you're not bringing snacks to the party, don't come. Periodt."

Tip: Adding a hand flip or snapping gesture enhances the delivery.

Petty (adjective)

Definition: Describes someone who is being deliberately minor, trivial, or overreacting to small annoyances—usually in a funny way.
Usage: For situations where someone's making mountains out of molehills.

Examples:
"She unfriended him just because he liked her friend's post. Petty."
"I brought cookies to the potluck because she said I couldn't bake. Petty queen."
Category – Related Phrase:
Petty King/Queen: A title for someone who excels at being delightfully spiteful.

Pop Off (phrase)

Definition: To go above and beyond, excel, or make an impressive statement. Can also mean getting passionately expressive in a heated moment.

Usage: For someone who's crushing it or letting their emotions fly.

Examples:
"Her performance last night? She really popped off."
"You're upset about that text? Pop off, I guess."
Tip: Can be sarcastic when someone's being unnecessarily dramatic.
Example: "Yelling over spilled milk? Pop off."

Pretty Privilege (noun)

Definition: The perceived benefits or advantages someone receives due to their attractiveness.
Usage: Often used to call out how looks can open doors—fairly or unfairly.

Examples:
"She got free drinks at the club again? That's pretty privilege."
"Pretty privilege is real—I asked for ketchup, and they gave me fries too."
Fun Fact: While it's often used jokingly, it also sparks serious conversations about societal biases.

Pog (adjective/interjection)

Definition: A gaming term that evolved into an expression of excitement or approval. Short for "play of the game."
Usage: Use it to hype up something cool or unexpected.

Examples:
"You found $20 in your pocket? Pog!"
"She aced her exam without studying? That's so pog."
Fun Fact: Originally popularized in gaming streams on Twitch, "pog" now thrives as a universal term for "epic win."

Q

Quiet Quitting (noun/verb)

Definition: Doing only what's required at work—no more, no less—without formally resigning. It's setting boundaries, not burning bridges.
Usage: Perfect for describing work-life balance rebellion.

Examples:
"I stopped staying late at work. I'm officially quiet quitting."
"He's quiet quitting by ignoring all emails after 5 PM."

Fun Fact: While the phrase sounds dramatic, it's really about taking back your personal time.

Quaking (verb)

Definition: Being so shocked, surprised, or overwhelmed that it feels like your whole world is shaking.
Usage: For moments when regular surprise isn't enough.

Examples:
"When I saw her outfit, I was quaking. She looked amazing."
"Did he really just propose at the mall? I'm quaking."
Tip: Pair with exaggerated emojis like 😱 for the full dramatic effect.

Queen (noun)

Definition: A term of empowerment, respect, or admiration for someone (regardless of gender) who is thriving or serving major energy.
Usage: Use it to hype someone up or recognize their greatness.

Examples:

"You aced that test? Go off, queen!"
"Her dance moves last night were unreal. She's a queen."
Category — Variations:
Slay Queen: Someone who's excelling at life.
Example: "She's running this meeting like a slay queen."

Questionable (adjective)

Definition: A polite way of saying something is suspicious, weird, or outright bad.
Usage: Often used as a diplomatic roast.

Examples:
"That haircut? Questionable at best."
"Your decision to wear socks with sandals is... questionable."
Fun Fact: "Questionable" lets you criticize while keeping the peace—it's the passive-aggressive queen of slang.

Quit Playing (phrase)

Definition: A way to tell someone to stop joking, lying, or messing around.
Usage: Throw it out when you need someone to get serious.

Examples:

"You got tickets to Taylor Swift? Quit playing!"
"He said pineapple doesn't belong on pizza? Quit playing."

Tip: Add a playful smirk to keep it lighthearted, unless you're actually mad.

Quick Flex (phrase)

Definition: A subtle or casual way of showing off something impressive without making it a big deal. Usage: For those moments when you can't help but highlight your wins.

Examples:
"I just finished a 10K run. Quick flex."
"Oh, this vintage jacket? Found it for $10. Quick flex."
Category – Reverse Flex:
Self-deprecating flexes also count.
Example: "Forgot my wallet but got free coffee anyway. Quick flex."

R

Rizz (noun/verb)

Definition: Charisma or charm, especially in the context of flirting or attracting others. To "have rizz" is to effortlessly woo people.
Usage: Used to compliment someone's game—or lack thereof.

Examples:
"He's got no rizz. He just keeps saying, 'You up?'"
"Did you see how she made him laugh? Ultimate rizz."
Fun Fact: Short for "charisma," because Gen Z refuses to use whole words anymore.

Ratio (noun/verb)

Definition: When a reply on social media gets more likes or engagement than the original post, indicating the reply is better or the original post is bad.
Usage: A devastating insult on Twitter and TikTok.

Examples:
"That bad take about pineapple pizza? It got ratioed so hard."
"Someone tried to cancel cats, and the dog lover ratioed them in the comments."
Tip: Drop a simple "Ratio?" under a post if you're confident your reply will dominate.

Receipts (noun)

Definition: Evidence or proof, often in the form of screenshots or video.
Usage: For moments when you need to back up claims or call someone out.

Examples:
"You say you didn't text her, but I've got the receipts."
"The receipts are on Twitter, and they're not looking good for him."
Fun Fact: Gen Z thrives on digital documentation—always screenshot with caution.

Real One (noun)

Definition: Someone loyal, trustworthy, and dependable. A term of high respect for those who keep it real.
Usage: Use it to recognize friends who always have your back.

Examples:
"She stayed up all night helping me study. She's a real one."
"Thanks for letting me crash at your place. You're a real one."

Tip: Call someone a "real one" in tough times for bonus friendship points.

Running Through It (phrase)

Definition: Pushing through a difficult situation or a lot of tasks with determination.
Usage: For moments when you're handling chaos like a champ.

Examples:
"I've got three exams and a work shift tomorrow, but I'm running through it."
"She's running through this marathon like it's nothing."
Fun Fact: Often paired with a tired-but-determined vibe.

Relax (verb)

Definition: A gentle or sarcastic way to tell someone to calm down, take a step back, or stop overreacting.
Usage: Use it to defuse tension—or add to it if used with irony.

Examples:
"You're freaking out over nothing. Relax."
"I just asked for directions. Relax."
Category – Delivery Matters:

Calm tone = de-escalation.
Sarcastic tone = invitation to more drama.

S

Slay (verb)

Definition: To succeed, look amazing, or perform
exceptionally well. It's the ultimate compliment for
thriving.
Usage: Use it to hype someone up for absolutely
killing it in any area of life.

Examples:
"Your outfit is everything. Slay!"
"She slayed that speech. The crowd was in awe."
Fun Fact: Originated in LGBTQ+ and drag culture, but now
everyone's slaying in their own way.

Sus (adjective)

Definition: Short for "suspicious." Used to describe
something shady, sketchy, or just off.
Usage: Perfect for calling out weird vibes or sketchy
behavior.

Examples:

"Why did he leave the party early? That's sus."
"She's acting sus—what's she hiding?"
Category – Pop Culture Connection:
Popularized by the game Among Us, where finding the
"impostor" is the whole point.
Example: "Red is always sus."

Simp (noun/verb)

Definition:
(noun) Someone who does way too much for
someone they're interested in, often at their own
expense.
(verb) To excessively obsess over or idolize someone.
Usage: Use it jokingly to tease someone's
crush-induced behavior.

Examples:
"He waited in line for three hours just to buy her flowers?
What a simp."
"I simp for anyone who brings me coffee."
Tip: While it's often lighthearted, don't overuse it to
downplay genuine kindness.

Sending Me (phrase)

Definition: A reaction to something so funny or outrageous that it metaphorically transports you out of your current state.
Usage: For moments of uncontrollable laughter or disbelief.

Examples:
"That meme of the dog in sunglasses? It's sending me."
"He tried to jump over the fence and got stuck. I'm sent."
Fun Fact: Often paired with "to the moon" for extra drama.
Example: "That TikTok is sending me to the moon."

Stay Mad (phrase)

Definition: A sarcastic or dismissive way to respond to someone who's upset, implying their anger is irrelevant.
Usage: Use it to shut down drama or trolling.

Examples:
"You're mad I got the last cookie? Stay mad."
"They're still complaining about my post? Stay mad."
Category – Alternate Use:
Can also be used playfully among friends.
Example: "I'm better at trivia than you. Stay mad."

Spill the Tea (phrase)

Definition: To share gossip, juicy details, or drama. It's the modern equivalent of "dish the dirt."
Usage: Perfect for starting or continuing a conversation about the latest scandals.

Examples:
"Did you hear what happened at the party? Spill the tea."
"I've got some tea about her ex. You ready for this?"
Fun Fact: "Tea" originates from drag culture and refers to "truth," but it's now all about gossip.

T

Tea (noun)

Definition: Gossip, drama, or juicy information. Sharing the "tea" means spilling the truth in a way that entertains.
Usage: Use it to describe any exciting or shocking revelation.

Examples:
"I have tea about their breakup, and it's wild."
"She always has the best tea about what's happening at work."

Tip: Add "hot" before tea if it's particularly fresh or scandalous.
Example: "Omg, I've got some hot tea about that party."

Try-Hard (noun/adjective)

Definition: Someone who tries way too hard to impress or succeed, often to the point of being cringe-worthy.
Usage: Use it to roast someone putting in excessive effort where it's unnecessary.

Examples:
"He bought her a diamond necklace on the first date? Such a try-hard."
"Her TikTok has five hashtags and two filters—total try-hard energy."
Fun Fact: Being a try-hard isn't always bad; sometimes it's just misunderstood ambition.

TFW (noun)

Definition: Stands for "That Feeling When." Used to caption relatable or oddly specific situations.
Usage: Usually paired with memes, gifs, or exaggerated photos.

Examples:

"TFW you open your fridge, and there's nothing to eat except condiments."

"TFW you send a risky text and see typing dots for five minutes."

Category – Emoji Pairing: Often used with 🌚 or 🪦 to enhance the vibe.

Toxic (adjective)

Definition: Describes behavior, people, or situations that are harmful, manipulative, or emotionally draining.
Usage: For calling out red flags or bad vibes.

Examples:

"He texts me only when he's bored. That's so toxic."

"I had to leave that group chat—it was toxic AF."

Tip: Use carefully; overusing it can make you the toxic one.

Thirst Trap (noun)

Definition: A provocative photo or video posted online to gain attention, compliments, or likes.
Usage: Use it to describe someone flexing their looks for validation or fun.

Examples:
"Her beach selfie was definitely a thirst trap."
"He posted a gym pic with no shirt. Obvious thirst trap."
Category – Response Options:
Leave a emoji if you approve.
Say "smh" if you're calling it out.

Twinning (verb/adjective)

Definition: When two people unintentionally (or intentionally) look or act alike. It's all about shared vibes.
Usage: For matching outfits, synchronized actions, or similar attitudes.

Examples:
"We showed up in the same hoodie. Twinning!"
"Her energy matches mine. We're twinning in every way."
Fun Fact: Bonus points if you say it while striking a pose with your "twin."

U

Unalive (verb/adjective)

Definition: A euphemism for death or dying, often used humorously or to soften the tone in sensitive conversations.
Usage: For moments of frustration, exhaustion, or dark humor.

Examples:
"This math homework is making me want to unalive."
"He didn't water his plants, and now they're unalived."
Tip: Use carefully—dark humor isn't for everyone.

Ultimate Cringe (noun)

Definition: The highest level of cringe-worthy behavior, beyond repair.
Usage: Reserved for moments when secondhand embarrassment reaches its peak.

Examples:
"He tried to propose with a TikTok dance. Ultimate cringe."
"Her mom commented 'hot' on her selfie. That's ultimate cringe."
Fun Fact: Gen Z's cringe tolerance is lower than previous generations—keep it chill or risk the label.

Unbothered (adjective)

Definition: Calm, collected, and unaffected by drama, negativity, or chaos.
Usage: For people who stay cool under pressure or don't let haters get to them.

Examples:
"She walked past her ex with her new bae, totally unbothered."
"Everyone's fighting, but I'm just here sipping my iced coffee. Unbothered."
Category – Related Term:
Unproblematic Queen/King: Someone who's unbothered and avoids all drama.
Example: "Zendaya? Total unproblematic queen."

Upgrade (verb/noun)

Definition: To level up or improve something, often with a noticeable glow-up.
Usage: Use it to describe moving from mid to iconic.

Examples:
"I switched from instant ramen to homemade pho. Big upgrade."
"Her new hairstyle is such an upgrade from the bangs phase."
Tip: When in doubt, add ✨ for sparkle energy.

Example: "She upgraded her whole vibe ✦."

Ugh, I Can't (phrase)

Definition: A dramatic way of expressing frustration, disbelief, or exasperation.
Usage: For those moments when words fail and drama takes over.

Examples:
"She said she's not going because her nail broke. Ugh, I can't."
"My Wi-Fi keeps disconnecting during class. Ugh, I can't with this."
Fun Fact: Saying it while rolling your eyes enhances the effect.

Unironically (adverb)

Definition: To emphasize that something is done or liked without sarcasm or mockery, even if it seems uncool.
Usage: Use it when you genuinely enjoy something most people might consider cringe.

Examples:
"I unironically love watching old Disney Channel movies."

"He unironically listens to elevator music and enjoys it."
Tip: Use sparingly—too much unironically and you might become ironically cringe.

V

Vibes (noun)

Definition: The overall atmosphere, energy, or feeling of a situation, person, or place.
Usage: Use it to describe anything from a party's energy to someone's aura.

Examples:
"This playlist is giving summer vibes."
"The coffee shop's vibes were off—too bright and no music."
Fun Fact: Pair with "good" or "bad" for instant mood clarification.
Example: "Her smile gives good vibes only."

Vibing (verb)

Definition: Relaxing, enjoying, or harmonizing with the moment. Think of it as living your best life in that specific instant.

Usage: For chilling, hanging out, or enjoying an atmosphere.

Examples:
"We were just vibing at the beach all day."
"This song comes on, and I'm instantly vibing."
Tip: Add "hard" for extra emphasis.
Example: "I'm vibing hard to this beat."

Valid (adjective)

Definition: Legitimate, cool, or acceptable. A stamp of approval for something or someone.
Usage: Use it when someone deserves respect or their opinion hits the mark.

Examples:
"Her style is so valid. She knows what's up."
"That's a valid reason to cancel plans. Self-care first."
Category – Opposite Term:
Invalid: For roasting bad takes.
Example: "Saying pineapple on pizza is gross? Invalid opinion."

Vanilla (adjective)

Definition: Basic, bland, or lacking excitement. Can describe anything from a person to an idea.
Usage: Perfect for calling out things that are too safe or unoriginal.

Examples:
"His playlist is so vanilla. It's all top 40 hits."
"Their date idea was dinner and a movie. How vanilla."
Fun Fact: While it's usually an insult, some people proudly embrace their vanilla vibes.

Venmo Me (phrase)

Definition: A direct (sometimes joking) way to ask for money or split expenses.
Usage: Works for actual reimbursements or as a playful demand.

Examples:
"You ate half my fries. Venmo me $2."
"Venmo me $5 for gas, or I'm leaving you here."
Tip: Pair with a laughing emoji to soften the demand.
Example: "You made me cry laughing—Venmo me for emotional damages ●."

Villain Era (noun)

Definition: A phase in which someone stops being overly nice or accommodating and prioritizes their own needs unapologetically.
Usage: Use it to describe a bold personal rebrand.

Examples:
"She stopped answering her ex's texts. Total villain era vibes."
"I'm saying no to everything I don't want to do. Welcome to my villain era."
Fun Fact: Being in your villain era doesn't mean you're evil—just setting boundaries like a boss.

W

W (noun)

Definition: A win, success, or victory. The opposite of an "L" (loss).
Usage: Use it to celebrate a personal achievement or commend someone else's triumph.

Examples:
"I got tickets to the Taylor Swift concert. Huge W!"
"You finally passed that class? That's a W for sure."
Category – Variations:
Big W: For monumental wins.

Example: "She landed her dream job. Big W!"
Walking W: Someone who's consistently winning.
Example: "She's so talented and kind—an absolute walking W."

Woke (adjective)

Definition: Socially aware, informed, or aligned with progressive values. Originally used to describe being "awake" to injustice but now often used sarcastically.
Usage: For calling out awareness or, in some cases, performative activism.

Examples:
"She's so woke about environmental issues. She even composts."
"Oh, you just discovered wage inequality? Welcome to being woke."
Fun Fact: Once purely positive, it's now occasionally used ironically to critique over-the-top "awareness."

Wildin' (verb)

Definition: Acting recklessly, saying outrageous things, or just being over-the-top in any way.
Usage: Use it to call out chaotic behavior.

Examples:

"He jumped in the pool with his clothes on. He's wildin'."

"You ate 10 tacos in one sitting? Wildin' for real."

Category – Levels of Wildin':

Mildly wildin': Unexpected but funny.

Fully wildin': Complete chaos.

Example: "Stealing the mic at karaoke? Fully wildin'."

Wholesome (adjective)

Definition: Genuinely kind, heartwarming, or pure. Often used to describe feel-good moments or people.

Usage: For anything that makes you smile or restores your faith in humanity.

Examples:

"Their friendship is so wholesome. They always hype each other up."

"That video of a grandma learning TikTok is the most wholesome thing I've seen all week."

Fun Fact: "Wholesome" became a meme as a counter to the usual internet chaos.

Weird Flex, But Okay (phrase)

Definition: A sarcastic response to someone bragging about something unusual, irrelevant, or unnecessary.
Usage: Perfect for roasting humblebrags or odd statements.

Examples:
"He said he owns 47 pairs of Crocs. Weird flex, but okay."
"She bragged about knowing the quadratic formula. Weird flex, but okay."
Tip: Works best with a slightly amused tone—keep it playful.

Winning (adjective)

Definition: Thriving, succeeding, or having a good streak of positive outcomes.
Usage: Use it to describe moments of momentum or general excellence.

Examples:
"I aced my exam and got a free coffee this morning. I'm winning today."
"They dropped an album and announced a tour on the same day. They're winning."
Category – Opposite Term:
Losing: For when the vibes aren't immaculate.

Example: "Lost my keys and spilled my drink—definitely losing today."

X Games Mode (phrase)

Definition: Acting or performing at an extreme, reckless, or over-the-top level, often humorously.
Usage: Use it to describe wild or intense actions, even if they're exaggerated.

Examples:
"He climbed the fridge to get cookies. Dude's on X Games mode."
"She turned a paper airplane into a dart. X Games mode activated."
Fun Fact: The phrase became iconic after a viral Vine, proving Gen Z's love for dramatics.

XD (emoji-like)

Definition: A laughing face emoticon from the early days of the internet. Now used ironically to mock outdated humor or old-school internet culture.
Usage: Perfect for poking fun at cringey jokes or nostalgic moments.

Examples:
"Remember when everyone used XD in chat? So embarrassing XD."
"I still say lol XD unironically. Fight me."
Tip: Only use if you're in on the joke—or ready to embrace your inner millennial.

Y

Yeet (verb/interjection)

Definition: To throw something with force or enthusiasm, or to express excitement and emphasis. Usage: It works for both physical actions and verbal reactions.

Examples:
(Physical) "He yeeted his phone across the room when he got mad."
(Emotional) "The teacher just canceled the test! Yeet!"
Fun Fact: Yeet started as a dance move but evolved into a versatile expression for all things energetic.

Yikes (interjection)

Definition: A reaction to something awkward, embarrassing, or cringey. It's like saying "oof" but with more judgment.

Usage: For calling out bad vibes or secondhand embarrassment.

Examples:

"They tried to rap during the presentation? Yikes."

"Her outfit clashed so hard with the theme. Big yikes."

Category – Levels of Yikes:

Small Yikes: Mildly awkward.

Big Yikes: Fully cringe-worthy.

Example: "Singing off-key at karaoke? Big yikes."

YOLO (phrase)

Definition: Short for "You Only Live Once." A rallying cry for taking risks or living in the moment.

Usage: Use it before making questionable decisions you'll later justify.

Examples:

"I booked a spontaneous trip to Paris. YOLO!"

"Skipping class to go to the concert? YOLO vibes."

Fun Fact: YOLO peaked in the 2010s but still pops up when you need an excuse for impulsive fun.

You're Him/Her (phrase)

Definition: A compliment to someone who's thriving, excelling, or embodying greatness. "Him" or "Her" refers to the person everyone admires.
Usage: For hyping up someone's standout moment.

Examples:
"Scoring that winning goal? You're him."
"She walked into the party and owned it. She's her."
Category – Expansion: Add "for real" to amplify.
Example: "You're him for real. Don't let anyone tell you otherwise."

Z

Zoomies (noun)

Definition: A burst of hyperactive energy, usually referring to pets but also applies to humans in chaotic moments.
Usage: For those times when someone—or something—can't sit still.

Examples:
"My dog gets the zoomies every night at 9 PM."

"She drank three Red Bulls and now has the zoomies in the office."
Fun Fact: Pets perfected it, but humans in sugar rush mode took it to the next level.

Zaddy (noun)

Definition: A confident, attractive, and stylish man, usually with an air of authority or charm.
Usage: Use it to compliment someone who's hot but also has "boss energy."

Examples:
"Did you see him in that suit? Total zaddy."
"Jeff Goldblum is the definition of a zaddy."
Tip: Not to be confused with "daddy," though the overlap is undeniable.

Zero Chill (phrase)

Definition: A state of having no restraint, patience, or subtlety. Often used to call out overly dramatic or impulsive behavior.
Usage: Perfect for describing people who take things too far.

Examples:

"He told her he loved her on the first date? Zero chill."
"They made memes about the breakup 10 minutes after it happened. No chill."
Category – Opposite Term:
Full Chill: Rare but possible.
Example: "He handled that argument with full chill. Impressive."

Zzz (noun/emoji-like)

Definition: A playful way to indicate boredom, disinterest, or sleepiness.
Usage: For moments when you're underwhelmed or genuinely ready to nap.

Examples:
"Another story about their vacation? Zzz."
"We've been in this lecture for two hours. Zzz."
Tip: Perfect for roasting without saying much—brevity is key.

Made in the USA
Monee, IL
10 December 2024

73273836R00049